The Pyramid of Love and Gratitude & The Laws of the Universe

By Melinda Pearce

ISBN # 9780615389882

The Pyramid of Love and Gratitude & The Laws of the Universe.

By Melinda Pearce

Edited by Risa Reynolds

Formatted by Joseph Rivers

ISBN # 9780615389882
Copyright © Chancellor Pyramid Publishing LLC. 2010
www.chancellorpryramid.tripod.com

The Pyramid of Love and Gratitude & The Laws of the Universe

Contents

Introduction

The Pyramid of Love and Gratitude was written to help individuals become aware of the power of the mind and to understand the true meaning of love and gratitude. This book is intended to act as a staircase leading upward to a higher level of thinking and behavior that utilizes the unlimited power and energy of the mind and the Universe to live a life of unity. This writing not only honors the African race, but also all who desire to learn the true reason for mankind's existence. Get ready to open your Mind to all the possibilities of your new future!

The Pyramid of Love and Gratitude & The Laws of the Universe

~1~

The Missing Link

It was not until after decades of confusion and asking "Why was I ever born?" or "Why was I even here on this planet?" that I finally began to understand what living was all about. Like many abused children, I endured a childhood of violence and anger and its damaging effects impacted me well into adulthood.

I lived a life of not knowing or fully experiencing the most important emotion a child should have from the very beginning of life. What I should have been taught was the meaning of certain four-letter word...that all-important word...if you don't know it and are deprived of it, then life has cheated you. You know the word I am sure...it is... L-O-V-E. I am certain that I am not the only one who did not experience this vital element -

the fundamental emotion that was missing during most of my life.

I survived my childhood and after I grew up, I became a mother and had five children -- and was determined to treat them differently than I was treated as a child. I showed my children love and I cared for them with all I had. However, I continued to live a life of confusion, wondering why I was always in unhappy situations. I never stayed in a relationship for long... seven marriages and seven divorces can attest to that. As I approached middle-age, I began to experience strange feelings from within, like a constant sense of loss or sadness, and that I was suppose to know something but I just couldn't grasp it. This weirdness was constant and I could only escape it with sleep or alcohol. I discovered that after I drank a couple glasses of wine, this dark cloud would encompass me, would disappear and that was a relief, but only temporary.

I tried many things to find out what it was that I was missing and supposed to know, but every attempt I made, failed.

If you can imagine what it is like to look for something and you have no idea what it is, it can be very frustrating to say the least. I changed careers from cosmetology to real estate, thinking perhaps that would help me find some answers. This was not the solution and I actually felt worse than before. Then I thought maybe relocating to another town, more in the country, was what I needed. So I sold my house and moved. That too, did not get me any closer to the truth. It was not long before I started to think I was going crazy and I was losing my mind.

One positive result of my relocation into a more rural community was that now I was living closer to my Uncle Bubby and his family. Uncle Bubby was my father's brother and was married with grown children, all of whom I had not seen for

25 years. I decided to reconnect with them and plan a visit. However, I never imagined that it would be my cousin's funeral that would serve as our first reunion. It was just two weeks after I had decided to reconnect with my relatives that my father called me to tell me that my cousin Connie passed away. It was unbelievable that I was going to see everyone again under such awful circumstances.

I attended the funeral with my daughter Tiffany and her son Junior. The last time I saw any of my cousins I was 16, and now I was 42. That is a huge time in between. I spotted a girl that looked like my cousin Donnie, the sister of my deceased cousin. She was looking at me, as I was looking at her. When we came face-to-face, I realized that it was not Donnie, but her daughter Tammy, instead. The resemblance was remarkable. Of course I was glad to see Tammy, but I was still also hoping to see her mother Donnie.

While we waited, Tammy and I spent the next four hours talking and sharing our life experiences. I spoke frankly to Tammy, who was 32 at the time, and I admitted to having constant, strange feelings and that it was driving me crazy. Tammy immediately and strongly reassured me and said, "You're not crazy. You need to get The Secret (by Rhonda Byrne) and listen to it." I had no idea what she was talking about. When I asked what it was, all she told me was to get it and listen to it that it would answer all of my questions. I purchased the CD version of The Secret.

Three days later, when I finally had some peace and quiet, I sat and listened to the audio. At first, my past flashed before me and I began to understand what I was doing wrong and how my state of mind brought all of the unfortunate situations to me.

I was still experiencing that weirdness as I always did. However, I noticed that the strange feeling was not as intense as before.

I continued to listen to those CDs every chance I got. Several months had passed, and I made progress feeling stronger every day. I continued to listen and never gave up on finding out what it was that I was missing.

The day finally came after months of relentless study. I suddenly was feeling very different. A strong surge of energy shot through me at an intense level, and I began to cry. I felt a sense of completeness at that moment sheer bliss. This was a feeling I had never experienced, and finally after 42 years, I discovered and finally found the missing piece of the puzzle! I realized that what I had been missing all these years was the lack of believing in myself and knowing my self worth.

It was not until this moment that I understood the connection to that very important part of who I am. From that moment, I was free and the world had lifted off of my shoulders.

~2~

Dreams

Within days after my earth-shattering realization, I had a vivid dream. It was so realistic that it replayed through my head the following morning as if I had seen it performed on a stage. I described the dream to my daughter Tiffany the next morning. In my dream, a voice instructed me to build "the pyramid of love and gratitude in honor of African Americans past, present, and to eternity." The voice also said the colors will be black, white and gold. The black must start at the bottom and go up at an angle to the top and then the white with the gold to follow. Those were the complete instructions. The part that was missing in my dream was the instructions of what material that would best be suited for such a grand Pyramid. Tiffany and I began to consider every way possible to make this Pyramid.

Within three days, I had another dream. This time when I woke up, I could not remember it, but I was left with the sense of its importance. No matter how hard I tried to recall it I just could not remember the message of that particular dream. So I let it go and the next night, the same dream returned. This time I tried in my sleep to make a mental note to remember it. However, the next morning it was lost again. I knew I had the same dream, but I just could not recall it. Right away I promised God to give me one more chance and that I would wake up and write it down. Sure enough, the same dream returned, and as soon as the voice was finished speaking, I woke up. It was 3:37 a.m. I hurried into the kitchen where I purposely placed a notepad the night before. This time I was ready to record the dream. I wrote, "Only when you open your heart to the love that has been waiting for you in the Universe, only then will you understand the true meaning of life and living."

That was the second dream but it was the third time it came to me and I am convinced that the number 3 plays a role in all of what I have experienced. I will explain more about this theory later.

In the meantime, Tiffany and I continued to brainstorm ways to create this pyramid, and no one who we spoke to could give any answers as to what would be the proper construction material. The only thing I could think of was to register it with the U.S. trademark office. I continued to go about my business and continued to think less frequently about the dream. I thought it was a nice dream but that was all it was -- a nice dream. Soon I didn't give it any more thought. Not long after my dreams, it was announced that an African American man, Barack Obama, had entered the presidential race. I wondered if this Pyramid had any connection to this historical event.

I was not sure, although I thought the timing was bizarre, to say the least.

I was still high on believing in myself and I was feeling really great for the first time ever in my life.

I started to read all the books I could get my hands on. I never use to like to read, but now it was different -- I was reading for a purpose. I had all of the books of the world to enjoy now.

I soon was in the mindset of moving back home to Orlando, but my husband wanted to stay in the little trucking town where we lived. I was okay with that plan, until the day a man appeared at my door delivering legal documents from Polk County, Florida. The papers were to inform me that the owner of the house we were renting from was in foreclosure and the mortgage payment was past due.

This was bad news for the homeowner, but good news for me. This would become my one way ticket back home. My husband insisted upon staying and renting a condo, so I decided to move back to Orlando without him and rebuild my life as well as my former cosmetology business. I moved home to my Mom and Pop's place and began to reassemble my life. Each day I was stronger and more aware of not only my inner vibration, but the vibration of those around me. I vowed to remain in touch with my cousin Tammy. I credit her with basically saving my life and steering me in the direction that I was so desperate to find. One weekend we met in Cassadaga, a spiritual camp in Central Florida, to attend church and hopefully receive a free reading following the church service. I was fortunate to get a reading by a woman who was a medium there and she began by telling me that I was "a kind spirit and that I enjoyed working with colors."

Tammy and I looked at each other in surprise because I am a hair color specialist. Suddenly, the lady yells out to me "stained glass!" I was not sure why the medium said that and she apologized to me as she admitted she did not know why she said that. She continued my reading and told me that when I was a little girl, I went in a different direction than everyone else. She suddenly shouts again, "stained glass!" and again apologizes and insists that she still has no idea why she said it. Once more she continues and informs me she is going to finish this reading and move on to the next person. She said, "Honey, I don't know what you have been doing but keep doing it. You are on the right path!" I gave her words some thought and the only thing I was doing was learning more about who I was and how wonderful it was to believe in myself. After church, Tammy and I parted ways once again and remained in touch, speaking frequently on the phone.

~3~

The Building of the Pyramid

As weeks past after my visit to Cassadaga, I was still getting settled at my mother's house and I found work at a "chop shop" - a low budget, high volume hair salon. I stayed as long as I could, while trying to endure all the bad energy among the women in that salon. I tired quickly of all the fighting among them. My whole life had been spent around family and friends that were in that mindset and I wanted no part of it ever again. After four months of mind-torture, I packed my combs and scissors and left to work in a two-person studio. My new boss was a breath of fresh air. She was strong in her Catholic beliefs and she was in a good vibration, which is what I needed to be around. About two or three months after working in her shop, one day as I was leaving work, and I noticed a sign a few doors down advertising stained glass classes.

I thought to myself, "that sounds like fun." I made a mental note and two weeks later when one of my customers was a "no show" and I had some time to spare, I decided to check it out. I went in to the stained glass shop intending to inquire about the class. After barely taking my third step through the doorway, I was overwhelmed with that same surge of powerful energy when my life changed for the better. I took a deep breath and asked the man standing there if he could make me a pyramid out of stained glass. He asked if I had a sketch and of course I did not have one. I had not proceeded any further than registering the pyramid with the patent and trademark office. The man said to give him a sketch and "we will see." I relayed my dream to him and the colors that it must have. I asked how much would it cost and he told me $350. At first, I thought that was too expensive, but I had to have it made so I agreed to pay $350.

As I was heading to the door, another strange occurrence happened. Something made me turn to him and suddenly ask, "How would you like it if someone had taken you from your country and made you do things you did not want to do?... and to someday get your freedom, only to learn that people still did not accept you?" I also stated, "Vision is a gift from God; and if everyone was blind there would not be any racism in the world, because you cannot hate what you cannot see." I was shocked that I had just spoken those words. It was as if someone else was speaking through me. I turned and left to go buy a few sketching supplies.

Once I had the material to draw the Pyramid from my dream, I went to the salon where it was quiet and I could work undisturbed. I started drawing as if I had been an artist my entire life.

I do not consider myself a sketch artist by any means, but I completed the picture on the first try, even though I had no detailed design, only the angle of placement of the three colors which had been stored in my sub-conscious mind from the dream. The instructions were to honor the three colors of black, white and gold; I looked at my completed color sketch and was immediately pleased with it. I rushed back to the man that was going to make my dream a reality. As soon as I walked in to the art studio, Rich (the artist) immediately told me, "Kiddo, I was going hard on you with the price and I have reconsidered and decided that I am only going to charge you $175." I was glad because I had bills to pay and I was by no means rolling in the dough. But no matter what, I was determined to find a way to have the Pyramid created. The man asked me to give him a couple of hours while he scanned my sketch into the computer and so I did.

He called me shortly thereafter, and asked if I wanted to see the design on the computer screen. I returned to his shop quickly and when I saw what it was going to look like, I started to cry. I don't know why I was crying... I just know that at that moment I was filled with joy. He reassured me that he would get started right away and that it would take a few days to complete the Pyramid. I was on cloud nine over the creation of this Pyramid and I knew it was to be of great significance to the future of the entire world. I was so high and felt my spirit floating, enjoying every moment of this sheer bliss of love and gratitude.

I rushed home and called Tammy and told her the Pyramid was being made as we spoke and relayed to her the entire sequence of events. Tammy reminded me that this was what the medium had been talking about when she repeatedly shouted out "stained glass" for no apparent reason. I was more convinced than ever, that I was headed in the right direction...I had no idea what was coming next or what was about to happen after the Pyramid was finally coming together and being created into something tangible that I could treasure. What happened next later that evening was the most incredible experience of all.

~4~

Another Dream

That night, I had another dream. Out of nowhere, a beautiful angel flew by me at a high velocity, and as she passed by, my eyes locked onto her. She stopped in mid-air, curved upward with her back arched for a moment and then moved gently downward in a floating, seated position and began to talk to another being, sitting in a forty-five degree angle from where I was. I followed the gaze of her eyes and saw sitting on a cloud, twin-boy angels. Immediately I became frightened that I had died and didn't say good-bye to my kids or grand-children. I remember jerking my head back and forth to force myself to wake up. I did wake up and was relieved to find that I was still alive. I did not know what my dream meant or why they came to me and I never even gave them a chance to tell me.

As I shared my dream with one of my clients, she thought that the angels were trying to deliver a message, but I had not given them the chance. I was sad and sorry that I forced myself to awaken in my dream. My client reassured me, telling me not to worry, and suggested that perhaps I had pleased God by making the Pyramid. God sent the angels to give me a message. She thought that maybe I would still receive the message, but that I would need to pay close attention to anything and everything that may happen.

Meanwhile, I waited patiently until I finally got the phone call from the art studio letting me know the Pyramid was ready and that I could come and pick it up today or tomorrow. I was so eager and anxious that I wasted no time going to the studio.

I entered the shop and saw the Pyramid sitting on the table and as I approached it, I started crying again. It was stunningly gorgeous and all that I imagined it to be. As I was in the presence of it, I felt the energy and the meaning of something very significant to this world. I paid the artist, departed, and returned home with my most prized possession. I definitely knew this Pyramid was meant for the world to experience, a message from the Divine Himself, with the infinite intelligence far more powerful than we could ever imagine. I placed The Pyramid of Love and Gratitude in a safe place in my bedroom.

Once I had the beautiful Pyramid in my possession, I still had no idea what I was to do with it or why it existed. I decided to launch a web site and place the Pyramid logo on it. The website is http://thepyramidoflife.tripod.com and I am proud of all the effort and thought that went into the site's creation. I also had to re-register the Pyramid now that it was in a three-dimensional art form.

I decided that my next step would be to research and study various topics for any clue as to what I should do next. I began by researching the subjects of Africa and the African culture. I studied slavery as well, which was tough and made me ill at the thought of what had been done to the African people. It was difficult reading, but I learned more on my own, than I was ever taught in school (which was nothing in regards to slavery). I found it interesting that the mission passage from Europe, to Africa, to America and back to Europe formed a triangle. I felt strongly that there was a connection to my Pyramid and that this was more than a coincidence. I also learned that President Lincoln's first and second attempt to free the slaves in 1863 were unsuccessful. It was not until the third attempt in 1865, when General Granger officially delivered, personally, the emancipation proclamation, to the slaves; The Proclamation of Emancipation stated that the slaves were to be freed forever!

I also researched the colors of black, white and gold. In modern Western culture, black has been the color most often associated with evil and death. Onyx is also related, and can easily be connected to a culture that was enslaved for 1000 years, to build an entire civilization. Although other races have been forced into slavery, no race had been more enslaved than the African people. In African culture, the color of black celebrates life, and the color white is most associated with mourning, which is just the opposite of our Western civilization. The color of white has also symbolized wholeness, completion and purity. Since ancient times, the color of gold has represented wealth and success and riches. The Pyramid of Love and Gratitude is composed of these three colors, that

are to lead you to discover your true self, and how to
live a unified life of happiness, health, and wealth.

~5~

The Law of Attraction

I knew that I could not embark on a journey alone to learn all I could, live the life I was intended to live, and undertake a mission far bigger than I could imagine. So I called upon God to bring someone into my life who could help me. A partner and a friend who was brilliant and open minded, drug-free, alcohol-free and who would love me completely. I vowed that if I couldn't have this, then I would spend the rest of my life alone. I meant it too. I was steadfast in my commitment to never again find myself with the type of men of my past, unsuccessful and hurtful relationships. I know these were my bad choices and I take full responsibility, because now I know better and I will have what I want or nothing at all.

One evening my eldest daughter Crista and her friend invited me out to go dancing. We were having a great time and suddenly I sensed someone near me. I could feel the energy of his presence, but when I turned to look over my shoulder, no one was there that I could see. It was a strange feeling. I continued people watching, but that feeling persisted. When I finally turned around again and looked further over my shoulder, a guy was smiling and waving hello, sitting at a distance away from where I was. I hurriedly turned away and felt embarrassed. The next thing I knew, that man was standing next to me and asking me to dance. I didn't really feel like dancing with anyone but us girls. I wanted no part of a drinking man which is usually what you find in a night club. I did agree to dance with my daughter and her friend. On the dance floor, that same guy was dancing near me and attempting to talk to me, but the music was so loud, it was hard to understand what he was saying.

The girls and I danced a few more songs and then returned to our table. The smiling guy came over and invited the girls and I to join him and his friend at their table. As we all sat down, he introduced himself as Joseph. I agreed to dance a couple fast songs with him before it was time to leave. The girls and I departed and headed home.

The following week Crista and I returned to the club and as we were walking in, Joseph spotted us and asked if I would please join him at his table and so we did. Once again the music was too loud to talk over, so Joseph and I moved to a quiet hallway, right outside of the lounge. I asked him if he knew anything about the laws of the Universe, he replied "no". I proceeded to tell him about my pyramid dream and all that had transpired within the past year. I could not believe how interested he was and he told me "he had finally met someone with something between her ears."

I was explaining the laws of the universe to him and how the mind is either negative or positive and sometimes in between, like I use to be. We conversed for hours and he told me where he worked. By the sound of the name, I thought he worked at a marina. Later, I had a chuckle when I found out he was a professor at Full Sail, a University in Orlando. The evening came to an end and I gave him my number and email. I was happy because I felt that maybe this time I had met someone very special and that this could be my best friend and partner I had asked God to send to me. Did I mention that the odds of meeting a man in bar who does not drink or do drugs are slim-to-none? But not this time – I felt my divine request was granted and I truly believed I had finally met the perfect guy. The following Monday I received a brief email from him, just saying a quick hello. For the next four days, I was constantly checking my email and text messages for any communication from him. By Thursday, I decided that maybe I had made a mistake about Joseph because of the lack of communication from him, since the night I saw him at the lounge. I laughed at myself for being so quick to think that Joseph was sent to me in the first place, even though he was everything I had requested in the first place. I vowed not to keep checking my phone and I certainly was not going back to that club ever again. I felt silly, even giggly, that I was headed down the wrong path yet again, (so I thought) and was thinking that this was just another example of how the conscious mind can play tricks on you. I released all the negative thoughts and went about my day. Several hours later, my phone rang and I see it is Joseph calling. I answered and he apologized for not calling sooner, but he had been working crazy hours. I was glad to hear from him and I agreed to go out to the movies for our first date.

I could feel and sense his great energy and I was drawn to him like a magnet. That is why it is called "The law of attraction." Our energies were in harmony with one another and we started seeing each other frequently and soon I was spending all my time with him - - so much so that my mom was feeling left out and angry that I met him.

Up until then I had spent my entire adult life always being drawn to the wrong men and settling for second best and for the first time I was on the other side and it felt wonderful! I was experiencing the positive side of life and everyday would prove to me that this is the way life was supposed to be. I was spending all of my time with this wonderful man who I felt strongly that God sent him to me and he was chosen to share this magnificent path with me and to help guide me through this magical experience.

Our relationship progressed quickly and Joseph would ask me if some day I would ever consider moving in with him. At first I told him that maybe we should wait because our relationship was so new and we had only known each other a short time. A few weeks past and I could no longer tolerate the negativity from my mother. Living in her house and hearing her constant complaining about everything, was taking its toll on me. I knew she was only acting out fear of being alone.

One thing I have learned is that once you have "crossed over from the negative side" there is no tolerance for negative energy. Not even from your family and you can actually feel it drain you, while trying to lead you down the path to self destruction. The mind is like a video camera -- always recording -- and it will manifest whatever it is taking in and the energy and emotions you feed it.

I finally realized that when you can't handle the heat, get out of the kitchen. Or, if you can't handle the negativity, remove yourself from it.

I decided to approach Joseph and ask him if his offer to move in was still open. He was thrilled at the thought of me moving in, so that is just what I did. I was determined that I was not going to allow anyone to destroy what I had accomplished or block the positive path on which I found myself traveling.

I do not blame anyone for all the bad things that happened to me in my life. I was brought up ignorant of many important lessons and I forgave myself for not knowing all that I should have. Fortunately, I have come to learn the truth of the spirit of not only God but Christ too, for they are one in the same to me.

The Pyramid of Love and Gratitude & The Laws of the Universe

~6~

The Pyramid's Journey to The White House

One day after Joseph and I were settling in and sprucing up the house, Joseph suggested the idea to send The Pyramid of Love and Gratitude to The White House. Several of my friends and family members also thought it was a good idea. At first, I was not too eager because I wasn't sure if it would even matter. It was not until someone whom I highly respected asked me to send it, that I knew I should. My mind was finally made up...I was going to send the Pyramid to our nation's first family! My immediate thought was to get another one made as quickly as possible, because I could never part with the original.

One day as Joseph and I were driving, a stained glass gallery caught our attention. We made note of its location and agreed to go check it out just as soon as we had more time. Joseph and I returned on a Sunday afternoon and even though it was closed, we wanted to look through the windows of the beautiful gallery. There were angels everywhere and lots of nature and animals. Our initial impression was that we had come to the right place. Three months later Joseph said to me, "honey, let's go see about the second Pyramid. Time is slipping away and we must get it made and sent to The White House." Saturday morning on our way to the beach, we planned to stop by to talk with the owners about making Pyramid number two. As we arrived at the shop, a sign on the door stated they were opening later that day. I told Joseph that we should go on to the beach and I would return to the gallery on Monday.

Monday arrived and I placed the sacred Pyramid securely in a box and headed to the gallery. I had no intention of revealing the true meaning and importance of my Pyramid because I thought it may have an impact on the price. I wanted to be treated fairly on the cost this time. I walked in carrying the Pyramid, introduced myself, and simply asked if it would be possible to recreate this pyramid, only with a cleaner and neater job on the lead lines. I also offered the blueprint, but the artist said she did not need it. She quoted me a price of $138 and I thought that was very reasonable. I asked if we could please get a handshake on it and she did. Then I said, "Great! Now I will tell you what it means and where it is going." I told her about my dream from two years ago and explained that the Pyramid is a symbol of unity in honor of African Americans past, present, and to eternity. I also informed her that the pyramid she was going to create was going to

The White House. At that exact moment, the artist's husband yells from the other side of the room, "Honey I told you I dreamt that our stained glass is going to be in The White House!" Surprised and perplexed, I looked at him, then at her, and asked, "What is he talking about?" The artist rolled her eyes and said that her husband had a dream several months ago, that their stained glass was going into The White House. She said that her husband told so many of their friends and family about his dream that she finally told him to stop because he sounded crazy. I knew at that moment that her husband had a special gift and he was able to perceive the positive energy that Joseph and I imprinted months before, when we stopped by the shop and touched the windows. I was in shock with the realization of all the people that had been connected to this mission and that there would be more to come.

I couldn't wait to tell Joseph about this turn of events. When I did, I think he was a bit skeptical. The artist told me it would be finished in two days. The day arrived and I invited Joseph to go with me to pick up Pyramid number two. After introducing Joseph to the couple, I intentionally referred back to our conversation two days earlier and I asked Mark, "So how does it feel that the dream you had of your stained glass going into The White House is going to come true?" He said it was a miracle and he could not believe it. I glanced at Joseph and by the look on his face he knew I was not mistaken in what had happened. After we got home Joseph said, "Honey, we can't send this pyramid to the White House...look, the design is not exact." He showed it to me and as I inspected it, I felt a sharp pain in my heart. I called Sarah and explained that her version was not an exact replica of the first Pyramid that I ordered.

I offered to return it and provide her with the blueprint that she initially refused. She did not want this one back because she had nowhere to store it, but did offer to give me a discount on the third Pyramid. I hurriedly returned to her gallery with the blueprint in hand and she said it would be completed in four days and "be worth the wait." I waited patiently for her call. The third Pyramid was perfect and even better than the original! She did an outstanding job and I was so thankful for her skill and care in the making of number three. It was indeed worthy to be gifted to the President of the United States. Before delivering anything to the White House, it is a requirement to provide advance notice. I sent my "letter of intent to ship" and waited almost two weeks before I decided enough time had passed and I felt the letter had been received by now. I wanted to ship the Pyramid to the White House in time for it to arrive by Thanksgiving in 2009.

The Friday before Thanksgiving, I drove to a nearby FedEx shop and showed the beautiful Pyramid to the customer rep and asked if the art work could be safely packed and shipped to arrive in time for the First Family's Thanksgiving. He reassured me that he and his partner were experts in packing such quality pieces of art. Before allowing him to pack the piece, I asked him to read the pamphlet I had written that was to accompany the Pyramid on its journey. I wanted him to know how important this special package was and the significance of it. As he started to read, he looked up at me and said, "Yes ma'am, I will pack this Pyramid carefully." I watched his every move as he gently wrapped the sacred artwork in three cocoons of bubble wrap and used three boxes strategically placed for support and protection of the diamond on the top. I was struck by the fact that he used 3 layers of wrap and 3 boxes; the care and skill which he used in packing the precious gift;

and the fact that he only charged me for one box. I knew it was no coincidence that I was directed to go there for the shipping of the Pyramid. On November 23, 2009, I shipped the precious Pyramid – a symbol of honor for all African Americans, with love and gratitude, to its true home – The White House.

The following Monday, I received the certified mail receipt that confirmed that the special package was delivered to its final destination. However, that posed a problem that I had not anticipated because I mailed a letter of intent to the White House nearly two weeks prior and I feared that maybe my package did arrive before the explanatory letter. I was correct when I received confirmation that the package arrived before the letter of intent. My third cousin Brittany and I drove to Staples to fax an emergency notice to the White House to inform them of the situation.

As the clerk dialed the number on her first try, she mistakenly dialed the wrong number. When she redialed the line was busy, she turned to us and said, "Oh, everyone must be faxing The White House at the same time as us!" trying to make light of the situation. On the third try (of course!) the fax finally went through. Brittany and I looked at each other and then I asked the clerk," How many times had she dialed the number?" The lady replied that the first time she dialed the wrong number, the second time it was busy, and the third time the fax was placed. Brittany and I just shook our heads, knowing that when it comes to this Pyramid, everything has been in threes.

In February 2010, I received a standard response that my gift had been received at the White House and a card of thanks had been delivered to me.

Not long after, Joseph and I were cycling one day and he asked me, "Do you realize that you sent the third Pyramid?" I had not thought of it until he brought it to my attention. The fact is that the number 3 has come into play on so many different occasions since this all started, that I believe it is significant. Immediately I thought of the Divine Trinity: The Father, The Son, and The Holy Spirit. The number three is significant as it applies to the Pyramid, because it honors African Americans Past, Present and Future, and is composed of three colors. It was the third pyramid, which went to the White House wrapped in three layers of protection, inside three boxes. I have spent, and will continue to spend hours researching and learning all that I can, to explain why all of this has occurred and what it means for us all.

~7~

The Memory of the Sub Conscious Mind

During one particular conversation with Joseph, he taught me something very important about the human mind – and that is, the human mind is a huge vault and it stores more data than we can imagine. Joseph explained that the dreams we have are often triggered by past experiences. He explained that maybe something happened long ago in my childhood that triggered my dream. Bingo! I immediately remembered an experience from my youth and the light bulb came on as I realized that he was right! I immediately flashed back to the year 1974, when desegregation was in the beginning stages. That summer, new school districts were being rezoned and some black children were reassigned to the school I had attended since kindergarten, Kaley Elementary.

As the start of the school term approached, I could feel tension building, but I had no clue as to why I was feeling that way. On the first day of school, I found myself among new peers of a different color. Before this time, I had never actually seen an African American; though I would often hear my parents speak about them. I did not know what to expect because the term "colored people" that was used in my house led me to the conclusion that they would look like the colors of my crayons - red, yellow and blue – the primary colors. When I saw these boys and girls for the first time, who were supposedly so different from me, I thought to myself, the only thing different is they look like they have been in the sun and have a dark tan. I immediately made friends with this little African American girl named Carolyn and we became best friends. As the year moved on, two African boys started calling me hurtful names even though I had not done anything to them.

This went on for awhile and I was afraid to tell my parents, especially my Dad, because he believed that fighting was a good way to settle disputes. And to him, winning was the only option. As a child, I remember him telling my older siblings that if they were in a fight at school and lost, then he would kick their behinds when he returned home from work. I had no intention of fighting the boys for calling me names, even though I knew how to fight. The only reason I would ever fight, would be to protect myself.

The name-calling continued and it was getting the best of me, so I decided to confide in my Mother, only after swearing her to secrecy not to tell Father. I explained that the two boys at school were calling me names even though I had not done anything to them. My Mom said in a calm voice, "Oh, they are just mad about slavery." "What is slavery?" I asked.

My mother explained the word "slavery" and told me that the boys' ancestors were slaves. I felt like a knife stabbed my heart because I knew this to be true. I felt awful and I was ashamed that my race was involved in this. I knew nothing as a child, but my heart broke because I could share their pain. My father's physical and emotional abuse to me and my sisters and brothers reminded me of what the white man did to their ancestors. I know it is not the same thing by any means, but you have to understand that from a child's perspective, living in an abusive home where you were treated like a servant and beaten if you did not comply or some-times beaten for no reason, it can make you act out of fear. These boys that were mean to me at school had been taught to hate the white man. My heart wept for them and all I knew was that they were only reacting to me in such a way to relieve the pain. Little did those boys know they targeted the wrong one, or did they?

The next morning, after my mother's talk with me, it was time to go to school and I surely did not want to face those two boys. The thought of skipping school briefly entered my mind, but then I thought of the beating from hell I would get from Father if I got caught, so that was not an option. I opted to have a conversation with God instead. I told God that I wished I could do something nice for the black people to make it better. I knew that saying "sorry" would not erase the pain in their hearts even though I had nothing to do with what happened to their ancestors. I told God that I could handle their name calling and that my shoulders were broad enough, because anything was better than an ass whipping from my father. With peace and love, I released my fear and I went on to school, not thinking anything would come of it. The boys continued to call me names and I ignored them until the day that one of them pushed me from behind so hard causing my neck to jerk back violently. That did it! I instinctively went into self-protection mode. My home life was nothing but beatings and I turned into a wild cat when Terry shoved me. I reeled around with my fist swinging and landed a punch to his face, giving him a bruising, black eye. I felt sad afterwards, and I was terrified that my father was going to be called and find out that these boys had been harassing me for most of the year. Luckily, that call was never made to my parents and those boys did not as much as look at me ever again. The year ended and school let out for the summer. I would not recall this experience until 35 years later.

Even though I knew about God from an early age, from the time I was 9 until I was 42, I sensed that there was a very important part missing in me and I had a strange feeling that was constantly at my back door. I often thought that I was a mistake and wondered why I was born to live a life such as I did, without love and support. It was not until my eyes and heart were opened that I realized that perhaps I was chosen to go through all that I did to be living proof of the power that is within us all. I have come to understand that we control and house the most incredible piece of equipment God ever created and that is our mind. Learn and understand all you can about your mind - focusing all your attention on it - and you will see just what I am talking about. Your master piece is waiting for you to live, love and be happy. Being full of bliss is God's intention for us all. Proper thinking is to believe in oneself.

~8~

The Meaning of the Pyramid

In retrospect, I believe that my passionate request to God and desire to "do something nice for the black people" as a nine-year-old desperate girl resulted in my dreams that lead me to create The Pyramid of Love and Gratitude. I continue to have dreams that contain very specific messages and I will share a sampling of them. These are the messages that I received in my dreams, in chronological order, during 2008 through 2010:

"You are to make The Pyramid of love and gratitude in honor of African American's past, present to eternity."

"Only when you open your heart to the love that has been waiting for you in the universe; only then will you understand the true meaning of life and living."

My angels returned to me to say, "Unity is happening right now, and for me not to worry about it."

"Cut the gray strings that bind you to the past -- your mind holds all the data to all of your past lives."

"Study all the words that start with the letters 're' because these words are in harmony with the Universe."

"You must trust in who you are and love yourself enough to fix what has been wrong for your whole life."

"The secret to freedom from everything is within your state of mind."

I have come to realize that my state of mind and my thoughts were the driving force of all that happened to me. The seeds that were planted in my mind as a child, and how I was taught to think and believe, carried well into my adulthood and really held me back. It was not until I became enlightened and aware of my true self and the powerful being that I truly am, that I was able to progress in life. I think the key is to dive deep into what it is real -- which is your inner self -- and learn how powerful you truly are. Never allow anyone to tell you that your shortcomings are "a gene thing" and "that you were born into the wrong pool" because that is a huge lie. It is true that the DNA that is a part of who we are. We are connected to the past as a result of our DNA. I now know how smart I am and I am working in full cooperation with the laws that govern this wonderful Universe. We all have the ability to change and learn a new way of life and living and the first step is to open your mind and eliminate fear and doubt. If you let fear and doubt take hold of your mind, together they will escort you into a short life. Be strong and stand your ground do not accept failure. Reconstruct your mind into success, you are worthy of that!

The Pyramid of Love and Gratitude & The Laws of the Universe

~9~

Love and Respect for the African People

Words cannot describe the love and respect I feel for the African people. The strength and pride they have for their culture, in spite of their legacy of having been enslaved, repressed and kept down for centuries, they have maintained their faith in themselves and in a higher power. From a young age, I always thought that what set them apart from other cultures was strictly attributed to their spirit and soul. Once I became aware and enlightened, I finally understood it was their inner strength – strength of mind and determination to hold their head high no matter what the circumstance. Their belief in God, and to never give up, is what makes them stronger. From their beginning, the African culture has been in communication with the creator of the Universe.

The African's were denied any education of any kind while in America. The plantation owners were mistaken when foolishly thinking that eliminating education would keep them in power over the Africans. As they danced and chanted, speaking in tongue was their way of communicating with their higher power and with each other. From that the energy shifted within the freedom that was present the whole time within their state of mind, which resulted in the freedom of their soul. If you ever want to know what freedom really means, ask an African American what it means to be free. I could not even imagine what it must have been like to be a slave. Although many slaves never experienced physical freedom, at least they had their most important and powerful freedom – freedom of thought. Fortunately, the power of their minds and thoughts could never be enslaved. It was due to their thoughts and energy, united for only one purpose, which made their desire a reality in America – the end of slavery.

U.S. President Abraham Lincoln is best known at the Great Emancipator - the man who freed the slaves in America. As the Civil War raged on, Lincoln regarded the war, "as a morale crusade to wipe out the sin of slavery." In a letter to H.L. Pierce dated April 6, 1859, Lincoln wrote, "He, who would be no slave, must consent to have no slave. Those who deny freedom to others deserve it not for themselves; and, under a just God, cannot long retain it." I will forever be grateful to President Lincoln for his bravery. He did not die in vain and gave his life for his country, his values, and holding steadfast to doing what was the Godly thing to do. I also thank and will forever praise our African Americans for all they have done for our country and for what they have taught us along the way. My mind and my heart are completely filled with an abundance of LOVE and GRATITUDE for the Africans for eternity!

~10~

The Future of the Pyramid

I will now explain what my goals are and how I intend to share what I have learned with the world. The Pyramid of Love and Gratitude is a symbol of Unity in honor of African Americans. This symbol belongs to the Universe and I believe it was God who used me as a vehicle, to bring it all together and deliver a message to the world of unity. The proceeds of the publishing of this book will pay to launch a line of clothing with the sacred Pyramid symbol as the logo. In turn, the proceeds from the Pyramid clothing line will start a non-profit organization named Chancellor Pyramid Industries. The primary goal of Chancellor Pyramid Industries, signifies an enrichment program and will serve to be an educational avenue for anyone who has the desire to learn the most important laws of the universe that are necessary to live a balanced and unified life of health, happiness and wealth. The doors of Chancellor Pyramid will be open to all who want to unlock and learn the laws that are already present within each and every one of us. You just have to start farming your mind like you cultivate a garden...providing nourishment and re-moving weeds every day to protect your investment and plant new seeds in the mind. This knowledge is worth more than all the money in the world. Ladies and gentleman, this knowledge is your birthright and no one should be paying to learn something that should be taught in schools in the first place.

My organization will coach you in how to live according to the rules that convey the true meaning of life. The formula is simple: Happiness + health + wealth = Unity. As you learn to live in harmony as our creator intended, your rewards will be unbelievable, to say the least.

There is no end to what you can achieve and accomplish in your life. Embrace a gift that is yours, without cost. Learning to live and believe in yourself is the answer for which you have been searching. Once you learn to transform your mind, you will have transformed your soul.

Chancellor Pyramid Industries is not an organization centered on religion or politics. These are personal choices and each person is entitled to their own beliefs. Our organization is here to show people how to create and live according to the three keys of unity. There are so many people searching for that special something that seems to be missing in life. As many others, I have discovered the universal secret and want to share it with the world from my vision. My goal and desire is for you to find peace inside yourself – and believe me, no matter how deep you must search inside yourself… IT IS THERE…. NEVER GIVE UP!

I define "wisdom" as the combination of patience, experience, knowledge and time. In order to accomplish your dreams, patience is required to undo the years of negative experience and burdens that have been placed upon you. Everyone has different experiences along the way and none of us are exactly alike. Your masterpiece is buried deep in your subconscious and it is waiting to be discovered and brought to life. You are a powerful and superb being and it doesn't matter what mistakes you may have made in the past that may be judged as "bad." I will show you how to let go of the wrong that you may have experienced or that may have been done to you. Do not forget your past experiences – just embrace them as wisdom and learn from them and know that they are essential in creating balance. By understanding why we act the way we do and making a conscious decision to remain in a positive state of mind, will produce good results.

Of course knowing this and approaching life in this way will not stop bad things from happening, but it will test you on the emotional level and coach you on how to react better and being in control over your emotions. It is always your choice how to react to trying times... the key is to stay calm. Reacting to a situation with fear, hatred or anger can carry a hard punch and can make a situation escalate out of control. As time goes on you will learn to control your emotions and believe in who you are. Once you achieve that, you will have mastered your life and become one with your creator.

This process will take some time, but not forever, it will take less time than it did to get you in your current state of mind. It took years to get you into this negative state of mind, and it will require some time and effort to reverse the damage. Have you ever heard "Rome was not built in a day"?

That means that great accomplishments do not happen overnight – they take work and persistence. It is very important to keep in mind, that PATIENCE and PRACTICE are the keys in learning how to rethink in a different way. The work you do during your conscious hours of wakefulness will be reinforced in your sub-conscious when you sleep. It is during the sleep hours that the wonderful sub-conscious mind goes to work effortlessly and will result in you becoming stronger every day. At first, you might think that nothing is helping or working -- and you could not be more wrong. Even if you cannot immediately see it or feel or even hold it, have faith and confidence, believing that the Universe is rearranging everything so that you have all you need to live in a unified, harmonious existence. Our creator intended us to live this way.

The more you begin to trust in yourself and who you really are, the faster you will see and feel the results of your hard work. Soon it will become second nature for you. It is essential to eliminate the fear and doubt from your mind and your life, and understand that how you have been trained to think from birth is incorrect. Turn away from conformity and the hereditary habits and beliefs they do not benefit you in any way, shape, or form. Soon you will realize how special you are and have been your entire life. Again, forgive yourself for any mistakes you may have made and just release them and let go of them forever. There is no judgment here. By reading this book right now, you are on the right track to discovering how wonderful you are. Embrace the wisdom of your sub-conscious and know that it has been a part of you that has been fighting for you your whole life. Now is your chance to learn all that you can and show the world all that you are and all you can accomplish by living in the consciousness with the direction of your sub-conscious. For the first time, open all your senses as you become more aware – and operate as a being of higher intelligence filled with confidence and certainty of your own powerful mind. Your mind works in harmony with the positive energy of spirit. Our job is to peel away the negative layer that has smothered all the good stuff and allow the positive emotions such as love, desire, and faith to shine through. These are just some of the Universal laws that are yours to study and master. In time you can become fully knowledgeable at the highest level – with your mind working at maximum capacity with all the senses and in full communication with the Universe. Knowing these basic laws of attraction, you can do and have anything you ever wanted.

For example, imagine a pilot flying an airplane. I have asked this question at least 100 times. "Who do you think is flying the plane, the Pilot?" Most say the auto pilot. "Who do you think activated the auto pilot?" Now what if we removed the pilot's brain? (which enables the mind to function) Now I will ask again, "who is flying the plane?" The answer is no one. Without the pilot's mind, the plane will crash due to loss of the invisible wires of communication that keeps that plane airborne. Think about that the next time you step on to a plane.

Before I close, I must share with you another experience that happened just before this book went to press. I wanted to have a vanity tag made for the front of my car with the Pyramid logo prominently displayed in the three colors of black, white and gold. Joseph and I found a business called

"Tags Are Us" owned by a man named Andrew. I approached Andrew and asked him if he could make the tag I wanted and also explained my dream along with the need to create the Pyramid precisely. I had a flash drive with me that contained all the blueprints of the logo for The Pyramid. Andrew said he could do it and for me to return in the afternoon. The material he uses is acrylic, which to me is very classy looking. He said the colors he was going to use were just as I needed except for the gold he proposed appeared too pale – actually more like platinum. The color he claimed was yellow looked more like a deep gold to us. After a bit more discussion, Andrew felt strongly that his gold would be the correct shade and that I should go with it instead. However, Joseph and I had our minds made up to use the yellow. Andrew gave in and said he would call us when it was ready. The time came and I was anxious to see the tag that he had made. As Joseph and I pulled into the parking lot and before seeing the tag, the thought crossed my mind that maybe I did choose the wrong color after all. Immediately, I felt that familiar feeling of energy surge through me and I then knew for sure I had selected the wrong color and that I should have listened to Andrew and allowed him to use his gold. I knew the tag was already complete and so I promised myself, I would use the correct gold color for the next one. I did not mention my thought or feeling to Joseph for I knew the tag was already finished…or was it? I asked Joseph if he would please run in and get it for me and so he did, only to return empty-handed. I rolled down my window and Joseph said, "Honey, you have to go in there! That guy is adamant about you using his gold." I said "You're kidding" and then I told Joseph of my thought and feeling moments earlier. As I darted into the shop, there was a group of people gathered around admiring the Pyramid tag being created. I explained to Andrew what just occurred and he said he really felt the significance of my story and he had cut both colors and wanted me to see them both. Well I already knew which one it was going to be - GOLD! This is just another example of how this Pyramid has a strong message and power and it will always be unique in its design. It has life now and it is a part of us all for eternity!

Finally, I am excited by the fact that I am able to share with you my experience and that I feel it is a sign of the New World. I think that we all are heading toward a new way of life, so get busy...you have lots of work to do, and once you have made enough progress, you can share your experience with the world. Reach out to the world --someone out there needs your help too in order for us all to come together as one.

Best Regards,
Melinda

The Pyramid of Love and Gratitude & The Laws of the Universe

Acknowledgments

This book would not have been possible without all the individuals touched by this wonderful experience in the making of the Pyramid. In order, I would like to share with you the chosen ones who were placed in the path of The Pyramid. Risa Reynolds, my best friend and the editor of this book, without her I would have not gone as far as I have. Risa believed in my experience and was a part of my life while it all unfolded and she too shares the passion of the message behind this beautiful piece of art and the journey behind the symbol of love and gratitude.

I am grateful to my cousin Tammy Pearce who led me to find the answers to discover who I really am and filled the dark void that nearly destroyed me. I also wish to thank my family: daughters Crista, Michelle, and Tiffany; sons Darrel Clay and Charles Norris:

Granddaughters Samantha Asha, and Arianna, grandson's Junior, Brandon and R.J, my mother Joann Grauberger; my sisters Elizabeth Thompson, Joanna Jensen, Melody Pearce and Anabel Johns; and my brother Wade W. Pearce Jr, and cousin "Lil" 3 Brittany. I also thank my extended family Joseph Rivers, Maxx Cyber Rivers, Yolanda Rivers, Joe Rivers. Diane Davis, thank you for being one of Cassadaga's most-gifted mediums. I couldn't have had my dreams realized without the talented efforts of artist Rich at Atlantic Stained Glass; Sarah and Mark at Stained Glass Gallery, Duane at Logo's, Mike at FED-X, Andrew at Tags are Us, Darcey at Boomerang Graphics. Also, my close friends, Vikkie Hankins, Cilla, Frank, Dwayne, Samuel, Anna and Camille – thank you for your encouragement.

Finally I wish to recognize, in loving memory of both of my dads: my biological father Wade W. Pearce Sr., and my "second" father Harry V. Grauberger, as well as my brother Clarence W. Pearce.

I want to express my complete love for both my parents and I do not hold them in any way responsible for how they raised me and my siblings. For if they had been taught differently, I would not have been able to share with you what I now know to be true. So thank you Mom and Dad, I love you both very much!

I open my heart of gratitude to you all for believing in this divine message. Without you all, none of this could have ever been. You all have opened your heart to love that has been waiting for you in this wonderful Universe in which we live. Thank you from the bottom of my heart my brothers and sisters and our holy spirit in God's name, AMEN!

REFLECTIONS
By Crista Ann McLeod

An entourage of thoughts and desires, combined
in a series of revelations that conspires
to bring us closer to the dawn of a new nation, to
expand the horizon and show the destination.
This is the time we must all reflect on our tribulations
and proceed through with no provocation
Leading the world through oppression and
depredation and healing the effects of mass creation
All of these things bring the hope for mankind, to
pursue our true purpose in life with a passion
Forgiving our past through procreation,
rehabilitating humanity with appreciation
Man, woman and child alike, all races,
all cultures will supersede this plight.
We have all helped to create
this magnificent light of inspiration
All roads lead somewhere and it is there where peace
and happiness dwells, within you.

1. Freedman, Russell. Lincoln A Photobiography.
Carion Books, 1987, p. 5.

2. Ibid, p. 135.